The Creation Frame

THE
CREATION
FRAME

poems by

Phyllis Thompson

UNIVERSITY OF ILLINOIS PRESS

Urbana Chicago London

Acknowledgments: *Shenandoah,* "Narcissus Walking"; *The Greenfield Review,* "Things You Will Never Have"; *Choice,* "Poetry," "A Note from San Francisco," and "I Have No Eyes"; *Quarterly Review of Literature,* "The Frames," "The Last Thing," and "The Municipal Gallery after Yeats"; *Voyages,* "Time Is the Matter"; *The Humanist,* "This Night"; *College English,* "Morning" and "More than Light"; *Poet,* "I Came Here" and "Molokai"; *Poetry Northwest,* "Waimanalo," originally published as "Weather of Heaven" under the pen name Phyllis Morgan, and "My Book"; *Arts in Society,* "Never To Be Cast Away Are the Gifts the Gods Have Given"; *Westigan Review,* "Feeling Erotic, I Go into the Blue Doll Bar and Try to Get Picked Up."

The author wishes to thank the trustees of Yaddo for the place, the time, and the peace in which many of these poems were written.

For Jerrie Squier
   from the beginning
and for Fay Reihl

Contents

Three

The Creation Frame
Ghiberti's Bronze Door

for Margaret Solomon

Adam, sleeping in the door, seems water.
He dreams Woman
And she becomes the issue of his dream, risen
From the sleeping vessel his body is.
His dream is nameless:
He has not said "Eve."

Her name still sleeps in the earth beneath his ear
And in the stream. It lives in air.
In the slung lines of her hair and his
It is cast
In the same passive swinging motion
As the water.
Eve is everywhere.

Her name will be his gift.
And evil.
Sin curves the smile of Genesis in Adam's sleep,
Waits on his lips.
He will say "Eve," and the name will be
Forever
A graved place
To know her being in,
A truer mirror than he
Though he seem water,
And though she love her image there
In him, in dreaming water,
Separate from God
Who spins above in a circle with a rod,
And separate from Adam.

"Eve."
In the tree they cannot touch
He hears her name
In the speaking
                    leaves
Eve
Needing to be gathered.

one

Forever
A graved place
To know her being in

Marble

Slung in the tide's large water arcs
My thoughts, turning back, sweep into the dark
Shale of the cove. Jagg'd. Loved.
Shot with ordinary quartz.

Shale. The color of New England coastal fog.
It looks like wet silk, feels quiet this time of year.
I think of marble, loved as well, cloudy as autumn sky,
And cloudlike also, though Leontes asked

What chisel could cut breath.

Like folds of bright wool, like transparent gauze,
Like wind-lifted linen, like the fingers of Kwan Yin,
Like Hermes' shoulders, like the hands of Jesus,
Like water, air, earth or fire. Like anything. And lustrous.

But Galatea's a myth, and Yeats' hungry lovers,
Kissing statues at midnight in some public place,
Kissed character into masks and went to bed.
Only Hermione lived, who never was marble.

Chide me, dear stone: You cannot.

O, I want something living, accidental, unearned,
A casual happiness, uncalculated, free.
I have grown sick of intelligence and measurement,
Of my own failings, sick of forbearance.

I want not to deserve what I have but only have it—
Life, the windfall, the flaking shale no sculptor needs.
I want my own lips kissed, my tears in plain pity
Rubbed from my face by hard fingers out of doors,

In such air, dim and brilliant, sun slow burning through clouds,
Lustrous, like marble. But not marble.
Marble is tragic substance. It is heavy.
Kissed, it does not live. It has no unresponsible impulse.

I am clumsy. I fail. I age. I am ashamed.
This is my only life. I waste in marble.

Potter's Cove

The same place.
Rain. Paint on my sneakers.
In iron water
The slick shale studded with barnacles
Seaweed and quartz
And I'm back again.

Well, what is it this time?
Here's rancor: Confess it.
More. I spit in the black wind my vinegar
Acrid with failing.
Do I have to come this far
With all that I have and always alone?
Hands in my sour pockets
The salt rain chilling my back
Under the flannel.
I know the lining.
I've borrowed this old coat before.

So what do I do?
I come back, I come back.
I walk on the flaking shale.
The Atlantic is icy and sweet.
Even in winter the gulls flap their big wings
And call over
Ocean water.

My Book

This death inside, my skeleton,
paces the length of days, winter
and summer, blind. It hears nothing.
It comes no nearer taste than teeth
packed in ruts of jaw. Odors
of buildings, meadows, streets, bypass
the insensible rods of bone I carry,
that carry me.

                How shall I touch them?

Wherever I go on earth or water
or on bridges thrust over water, or higher
than that, in planes, or beneath the broad
surface of things, in caves or subways,
what is outside reaches and fills
the cavities of my body, space
of the circling passages of ear,
warm places where my breath rises
and falls, all soft zones of love
or waste or sense.

                My darkest parts,
hollows invaded every time
and way I turn with different air,
keep their own secrets, are not mine,
are a new mystery, puzzling each breath
I take. Nothing I learn or love
is mine.

        The only parts that live
finally are the unknowing bones,
the anonymous spaces they define,
and this.

Read it.

At dead center,
to which my body hurries, bone
grins with a grave rhetoric, and waits.

The Frames

for Marjorie Sinclair

Wait here. Listen. Presences soft as snowdown
Are assembling, and you can find them becoming clear,
Can't you, in the window? Water glasses, ice tinkle of dinner silver,
Declensions of tone and motion tell how uncommon

They are in their ordinary brown dresses, eating apricots
And cheese. They will pull the mauve curtains against heavy sun
Only, against blanching, not to hide from us. In Dublin
It was the same—a lecture at Trinity, print exhibits

In Mountjoy Square, and thick plaster-painted crosses
Made of stone at the museum, after a gritty bridge
Over the Liffey. Worn walking to University College
Through Stephen's Green, I saw, cast through masses

Of high hedge leaves, a thrust of metal, and there
Strayed to some other celebrated Irish unknown.
But this was Moore's sudden bronze of Yeats fronting rings of stone—
That Olympian hurled single upon the astonished air.

There are some words a whole work is made for—true acts and names
That can't be written down. The mystery, *ḳaona,* makes me tell
Riddles, and what is not true I can say readily. Or I can tell
Crowds or strangers the truth. I take men without names

To bed with, innocent, but not friends, whose dangerous anagrams
Storm wth *ḳaona* and secretly punish me, a Spartan
With a fox in my heart, speaking for love to one man.
Untellable reality forever hurtles from frames.

Time Is the Matter

for Jim, Peter, Horst, Frank, Michael,
Dennis, Calvin, Howard, Norman and Mel

for all my students, my friends

In the highest room of the tower
where the season spills late papers
and late sun,
and a wind from the right side
rattles the louvers with cries,
our smiles lock to a stubborn line
and, distant by twenty years,
we find each other.

Oriental courtier, civil
and neat as evil, yellow tailor-learner,
with jacketed books and flaps to keep papers in,
clean car and handsome conscience,
though I tell over a paragraph
of your Japanese precisions,
I still cannot not love you.

Yet in this matter of love,
time is the matter.

The touch of your tongue in my ear
is quick as questions, warm
as the deeper English of your voice
inside where you hammer
ardent without the body of desire.

"Matter is an aggregate of images,
more than a representation, less than a thing."

Our minds lack matter for nailed memory.
Our love, that strums with answers from the world,
maps classrooms off anonymous corridors.

Nothing will ever happen to us
in backyards, beaches, and streets.
We'll never unkiss the barrier.

No matter:
lines of sweet English,
transparencies, frozen analogues of love,
pile up magnanimous images in safe time.
And time is the matter.

      *   *   *   *

I saw the massive shoulders of Poseidon
in ruined stone,
a rinsed fragment of God,
a solid light that brightened
the great gallery where he drove
love down my throat.

Heavy with the hard knowledge in my heart
I have stood at the grave of Yeats, raving,
wild with some kind of still, withering grief.

Narcissus Walking

for Donald Petersen at Yaddo
and in memory of Phillips Reid

The room is open. The shape of the room spreads
The space outward, wide. The walls carry the space,
Not close it, and the space shifts as he moves, gradually
Taking change and shape in the room where he is
Always alone. The windows open outward
Into the air outside and the encompassing green.
Standing, he watches the slanting rain. He hears
The rain splash over stones. When the rain stops
Later in the morning, he walks around the estate.
Rain still hangs in a sky as gray as stone.
Silent in wet sneakers, he walks down the edge
Of the grassy lawn, and takes the public way
To the rose garden, where the rose petals waft
The softest odors to him, the softest colors.
On the stone path he walks among the statues
And the stone benches, among stone columns, alone.
Then he walks through higher grass to the stones piled
Unshaped by men, moss covered, in a pool,
And receives into himself the stillness of stone
And water, in the midst of grass and moss.
Later, as he moves along the road
Into the open woodland, he is encompassed
By evergreen, by cedar, oak, and locust,
By arbor vitae, elm, white birch, and pine,
Their shapes and their substantial shadows. He walks.
Mushrooms grow in the moss, and on wet stumps
The fungus. Ferns brush across his legs
As he leaves the road. Mud sticks to his sneakers.
His eyes are open to the brown light of the slopes,

And he turns it inward. He sees the horsetail shoots
By the quiet lake, and he remembers beginnings.
He listens to the deep stillness of water.
He hears the distant stream rabbling over the rocks.
In the cold air his breath is moist. Is he
Alone here, at the center, held by the hard need
To know his own substantial form in stone?
He listens: No one calls or follows him.
He leans down and sloshes his hands in the lake
To move somehow into these outward shapes
Before he passes over the bridge and back,
Gradually, up the stone steps overhung with hemlock
To his own room, and to the open, the encompassing green.

Yet he seems, even to himself, to dissolve without words
In the shapes he moves among, the open spaces.

He is not here for long, but for long enough.

The Municipal Gallery after Yeats

i.

I've come.
The curved façade simplifies the cobblestones,
Doubles the ringing air.
How shall I shackle this clamor of gathering images
So I can slow pace the galleries
And let delight happen like ceremony?

At the door, abashed
As apparitions stream to mind, I falter
Toward a gallery of glass
To summon distance,
But there they are—eight "Irish Literary Figures."
The wet colors swim and blur, and I smile hard,
Hand gripping a kind of cold wood rail
To keep from being mocked by the hard Irish.

Their voices turn me out upon Epstein's bronze
Of an old woman
In whom I find that gaiety glittering
That brims Picasso's eyes
And steadies me against assaults of mockery.

ii.

Haggard, gaunt with some unspeakable emptiness,
She stares into her sorrow.
As if it had been my own, I remember.
Lifting my hand I touch her bound hair,
Trace the animal medallion at her ear.
How could you not love him
Whose celebrations mastered your stern comeliness?

Granting is easy: asking, so full of shame.
Can anyone now allay the dead grief
That hollows your eyes, lady?

My hand slips.
I remark the big portrait
Where, luminous with youth, she leans
To a pet monkey. She is amused.
She mocks the artist.
Love is a dress she wears indoors,
Chastity is a sash.

Wagons, great wheels, turn in the streets, spilling straw,
Drag angry queens, drag beggars through crowds, coughing.
She willed that. She could have been content—
Luck equalled her impulse.
But her crimes lacked sweetness, festive ease.

iii.

Sentences!
Who am I, with what authority come here
Before long-legged Yeats
To blame her in some phrase?
Authority of love,
Whose argument is thin enough, God knows.

iv.

Standish O'Grady's a handsome man, I think—
Blocked face like a stony challenge;
Douglas Hyde, his blue eyes brightening out of the canvas;
And in blue paint himself, John Yeats,

The sainted painter-father, late of New York,
His Willie a blur, mild as this John Synge.
Lady Gregory's portrait's creased—
Black silk barred and sunlight full of lines;
Hugh Lane—
    "Who's all them Yeetses, luv? If they didn't paint it,
    they're in it." "Come along, will ya, to the one that
    moves, Harry, all stripes."
Who's Irish, for God's sake?

v.

I can't see anything.
The flooding colors hammer in the air
And steepen, right and left.
The light spins. It's tangible. Does this room end
In an imagined Ireland?
If everything's remembered, when did it begin?
Stricken, I sink down, mantling my heart.
And this too was foreknown!
I am, myself, the imagined fact, outside of time, frozen.

vi.

Late afternoon Dublin's gray, all right, and dirty.
A cold sun dapples a plain memorial pool
And the Irish cram their benches, remembering.
Tonight, at moonless midnight,
At the dark where no human life is possible,
The stunned sky will fill with fireflakes again,
Deepening blue,
Trembling to stillness, free.

Ronsard Full of Sleep

Ronsard loved this body,
Bangled, cinnamon linen dressed,
Scarved in ribbed wool.
At my nibbled throat his jade glimmers.
It was he who gave it.

The vase is overturned,
Pours moonlight from its wide mouth
Over the terrace flagstones,
Spills lacquer down the rim
Among the wailing cereus blooms
Among the cups and dishes on the table.

Donkey! He bristles with paper.
New poems have knotted his joints.
Mon vieux, he can't do any more.
Ronsard, full of sleep,
Grown old in the praise of my body,
Nothing it costs the moon to enamel the garden.

Love in the City

Hard light, nailed into concrete,
Will plate me a halo tomorrow.
I'll stand in it, in front of it,
Making money indoors. And how,

Wearing that canny light,
Can I letter love free
Of error? Especially the sheet
Glass brightly burnishes me.

I'm clean type, smart as mail,
Fast as steel on a Tuesday.
Love, how can I tell
Grave love in the plane of day?

Can't you give me the studded air,
Midnight, weather of heaven,
Moon lilies, dreams in my ear?
Not you, no. When sun

Resolutely steeps ships, towers,
Domes, theatres, slantwise,
I'll have to hazard it. Hours
Of cranes and sidewalks, dies

Of iron, elevators, floors
Of my own corridors, all these
Will stir into gravity, when time pours
Softer shadows over us.

A Secret in Bone

Winds that have haled iced wires down
Collect here in a swirling sleep.
Snow, blue deepening in a swept oak,
And this flaking cold enclose what I've done.

The streetlight, soft gutter and curbstone,
Cars parked alongside the silence, ask
Nothing of me. I give them my keeping
Anyhow, without shame, for being common,

For being sure, like love wound in the marrow,
And last, at long last, and forever come back to,
But not easily, for forgiveness, this place in the mind,
This peace, the sweep of dark snow.

Morning

Streets drive the naming day into my eyes.
As traffic spills the riddles pulled from sleep
To fumes, the blue lifts them, and they dissolve,
Dissolve—wayfarers in seaweed light,

Sunburst of bicycles reeling over a rise
To the bird-stung harbor full of ships upon a map
Revolving—and the riddles drift, resolve
In the simple power lines as they spin and brighten

Into my real questions and the greenglass
Insulators, thick jewels on creosote poles:
Are you scanning meters of telephone wires?
Do you lean to the scoop of cables? Can you hear

The buzz of intersection stoplights, happiness
Of crosswalks? Love, do you turn to the clocking wheels
Of the cars, speeding toward reason, as I see the tires
Burnishing the highways? Hedges flare

With early morning. Windows burn to tile.
Eastward the boulevards shape warm, gilded pools.
Places! Identities! Can you perceive
The metallic gestures of day where I find you?

Waves release your voice in the sunny air,
Your name to these enamelled avenues.

The Desert outside of the City

Before this desert, this death of red rock, pronged cactus,
And the night closing us into it, we essayed
The city. And after.

But bless history that brought us here
Where we sense on our skins the critical breath of God.

Still, it would be as easy as it is false to say aloud
That in this desert our skins are both black.

Then what is darker? Him or the cold sky that widens
Over and at the back of the mountains?

We will leave in the morning by the same roads
That probed ancestral desert, knowing what we have known
And no more, under God's witness, but free.

For a Wrong Century

For a wrong century
Rain has been sinking into the charred rafters
That fell during the blaze, smouldering.
The house stinks,
Though this age the fire's been dead.
I huddle under burnt wood
But there's no getting away from the wet.
My sweater's soggy.

Still, there's no place for us but here—
You in your pale raincoat under the blasted pine,
Absolute out there, and patient as you need to be.
Your eyes are safe under mirror glass, involved,
As if you heard grave music
Folding like winding cloth around you.

The wet grass touches your ankles.
But the grass.

Even in dreams you deny me.

Naupaka of the Mountain

> Tearing in two the small white flower of the Naupaka, she tossed the halves away from her, one half to the mountain, the other to the beach. And she swore she would not come to her lover until the torn halves formed a whole flower once again.

Skin prickling, I will not lie down on beaded needles of ironwood
While the breath of a long wind hungers through the branches,
When the wind soughs in the upper branches,
I will not lie down with you.
The wind will talk with the clouds in a clear sky
But you will not come to the mountain.
As the clouds brighten above the paths where the wet seeds spill
Of guava—smell of sweet pink upon dust—
You will not come.
As the clouds are called over green gleaming bamboo
Above the knocking poles,
You will not come to the mountain.
Taut with names I'll rake my face on mountain ironwood bark.
Your arms will not bracket my shoulders,
Your fingers not snag in my hair's tangles
For the sake of a word.

And I will not come to the beach, past the ironwood break
To the cold edges where sea water slides on your ankles
And the salt air licks your ear.
I will not be light in breaking water with you,
Easy diving in images of ourselves
Colliding in the shallows with the backwash.
I will not swim deep with you
Released miraculous as a spear in the silky waters,
Nor wrestle your legs, damp in the stippling sand,
Since I will not come to the beach.

Till the halves of the white naupaka from mountain and beach
Are held together for the sake of a word
You will not come to the mountain.
I will not come to the beach.

Molokai

heavy into my shoulders
the cut mountain
  I did not know him
the simple shallows remembered
  mud warm underneath
  his broad hands
where the florid bougainvillea flares
orange upon kiawe brambles
  his hands
  widen upon my silks
  my inner thighs
  the flowers my breasts become
  open
the red earth is
in his hands
still
and I am

I Came Here

Before those azure water-swaggering faults
Opened to me, I reasoned like everyone else
In the North, where long windows filter celery light
In winter—ice air upon stone walls—and the quiet
Gropes inward. Holy names and words of the dead,
My own filming with them, stirred civilly toward God.
Ungiven, I shivered among them, before I came here.

I came here over the huge bulge and veer
Of the ocean, gapping out, breaking the roar
Of the planet, even. And it was not God—it was water
Sounding in my veins and in the unbalanced canals
Of my ears. It was myself. It was water and scrape of coral
In my flesh as I thrust myself to the rescue I have
Found on this bright reef.

                          Though the world's caves
And crusts are buckling, I cannot ever go back,
Pledged now to earlier mysteries. Red firecracks
In the fluid earth spit bolts of stone, flaring,
High piling over guard rails and roads. Where
Is the wall that will not melt in lava, the prints
Great waters will not drown? Things vanish, wince
Into elements, force them to flower—ohia lehua,
Kiawe, ironwood, hau, into humid air, scatter
Of dove wings.

                     Smoke odors thicken my throat, my hair
Blackens, and am I not honey-color, when fire
Fountains at the faults?

Waimanalo

I give this day to heaven.
Nothing prefigured it. It came safe
and suddenly, so without waiting,
that all I could do was stand wild
in the middle of it, allowing myself,
blown, as also the sheeted light was blown
out across wet sand.

This weather had no herald.
An unlikely wind poured down from the wrong side,
so this ocean rose at last
into my reach, cross waters driving
the salt spray of white waves cast
from breakers into the oblique rush of air I was held in
to suffer the sting of sand.

It falls to heaven's keeping
that was hailed in the rage of the lashed ironwoods
rimming the hard sweep of beach.
Sprung from loss, the time is untellable. It brightens
away. Now it's out of my hands.
So breaks the spare joy I was borne to—this day. Blessing,
I tender it. Receive it, heaven.

Manoa—Christmas

also for Nancy and
Bob Baird

Impact of silver!
Across Manoa valley
The wires spill
Out of slow light
And return quietly
To the poles of their other world.
Drifts of white mist collect, swirled
Low among the ironwoods.
Wet grass, wet fern blades,
Wet stems, wet poinsetta leaves
So still, this water silver
That makes the limbs wet.
Less than an hour since
We left the soft path printed
With our footsteps
And entered the mist.

A Note from San Francisco

Look—the first flower you find lovely today,
That one is mine for you.
Be happy. What can I say?
If I were there, I would bring it to you.

Fay

Fay, but for you, would the eloquent flare of hibiscus
I saw midafternoon
Fall to the grass have mattered less?
If not your caring, what was it inside broke open?

A blossom of such arrogant pain, paper
Curved in flame, red
Of a shame so pure
It sang itself innocent. What could you have said?

Or I, to a thrust of anther falling? It fell
This afternoon. This
Is midnight. Were I to tell
What shines inside, it would be loss and blessing.

Kauai

for John Logan, *out of our human love*

i. Kokee

This is not virgin wilderness:
Many kings, warriors, and priests
before us have listened
in the winds of these pinnacles
for a voice
ancient as the falls
and from as far a place
sifting through branched
ohia lehua rooted in the walls
and wrenched
over the chasm.

I give names to your questions:
This is the koa
whose leaves are like crescents of moon,
and that, lau hala,
with spidery roots
outspread to brace the trunk;
from its fibrous leaves
tough mats are woven.
Below, rimming the beaches,
ironwood breaks the hard wind
that blows from the sea.

But such names are not what you need
for the pain you keep
                having
to do with beauty
or gorgeous fear.

In that original wilderness
all words become
a flicker of syllables.
I know that friends,
a man and a woman,
cannot go into that huge quiet
together.

Go alone, then, go with love.
                                    Bring
out of that early forest
the Name you need.

In Kalalau there is a fall of water
that has no name.
I will stay there for you.

ii. Waimea Canyon

These moist rails—barriers.

The canyon spreads a silence huge and simple as the ocean
                    subsiding for centuries.

We more than plunge among juts and raw pinnacles,
Dream-tracing, like the sea, striations on red rock.

One bird rising describes the wide levels the sea fell down
Pulling from slopes and drops all the solving shades with
                    its white wings.

None of us remembers these falls of rock drowned
Or what heavy waters pummeled the lost chasms and made these
                    outer walls, these mountainous inner folds,
Which the sun distorts gently, casting light inside the rim.

History is not this red canyon where we shall not find a way
But ourselves near the falling road
At the rail here
Where you have kissed my mouth, John.

iii. State Park Cabin

We got lodged in there tight
Fronting the fire you made of damp logs
That hissed and sizzled in a stone place
But burned all night.
I said you were like Adam
Or some later thin-lipped saint I couldn't remember
Or a plain man
   your arms heavy as logs I couldn't lift
   across my back holding me pinioned
   as we stood barefoot on warm floorboards.
   It was the cold you held me from.
Thee is a loving man. Believe.
Thee is sent from God with good news.

two

A truer mirror than he
Though he seem water
And though she love her image there
In him

Never To Be Cast Away Are the Gifts the Gods Have Given

in memory of Hudson Bowne

i.

Staggered back, a scope of land stung on the sea
Shimmers in the distant haze of a dream, while noon
Brightens this slope of beach. I'm here for a reason
That seems to be losing itself in the spun green spray

I stare at, till images drown the mind. Love,
Is it? opens irrational inner landscapes
Where doing and suffering, dressed in the lonely shapes
Of themselves, become known. These regions are where I live.

Now, riding the dissolving surfaces of Earth,
The sea heaves reef-broken water upon the beach,
And the sand glitters to snow from the bare reaches
Of Hell, and the ranges of waste steepen in the North

Where nothing matters. My dead love, this
Is the slow seeing that turned your eyes to stone—
A leached plain level under a vacant sun.
In the teeth of your failed faith I hurled a promise

Made strangely from unbreakable spans of joy
Joining your death, my life, my grief: Never
To be cast away are the gifts the gods have given
That no one can have for wanting. I've cast away

Nothing yielded me, and this is for your sake,
For whom I wanted breath, for whom went weeping
To Hell, for whom came back without. I'll keep
The hard unequal bargain struck in the breaking

Winter—death for knowledge—though nothing I know
Balances your loss. Yet, love, what shall I hold
In the passes of sorrow? I wear integral cold.
The look in the eyes of the dead is worthless. Snow,

As incoherent as this endless sand,
Is what you gave me, after I had learned
To balance, mount and close in the burned
Arcs of your body, stayed by your taking hand.

Through your brown eyes outstaring chance and shame
I grew more chaste by changing the abstract gift
Of body with you, and you, more arrogant after.
And cruel, and young, I think, years later, naming

Your life with no less love. But I've known more
Than you, more summers than one, more falls. I know
They end on godforsaken streets of snow.
You would have left me, no matter what you swore.

ii.

And what could I then have believed in? But you died
Before you could be inconstant. As things are,
I can trust love, stay honest, speak. I fear
The collapsing sands and the veins of waste inside

That murdered you: I've seen them. But I'll keep
The promise raised against your early death,
Your broken word: As long as I have breath,
Though elsewhere in the world you lie asleep

And cannot hear me name them, I will praise
The lovely lives of Earth, whatever dies.
Terns in the salt wind. Though I've sunk my eyes
To levels below light, though nothing stays

I watch terns leaning on air. I'm here for a reason:
To speak truth with dry breath, to cry love
In the salt wind on this beach, in shame and grief,
To cry love in the blank eyes of death, love, and again.

A Late Snack

Midnight:
The kitchen table has quarrelled.
We lean on crude wood
Heavy with implacable emptiness
And nudge our cups.

This is bare anger I bring you, vulgar as shovels,
No pouting Dresden petulance in cheeks of sugar.

I'll tell you:
Whom love sufficed wants cheese,
Salt bacon and apples.
Eggs. Bread also—many warm loaves.
Have I ever asked forgiveness?

Listen:
What's called poetry dulls me.
The monotony of moonlight levels my head,
And I'll chew stale rolls tomorrow
Though you smile like soup.

Feeling Erotic, I Go into the Blue Doll Bar and Try to Get Picked Up

As I waken into this bar I feel
the bra feeling
tight
and my pants dampen
bar stool plastic leather where
dress cotton stops
and a ridge under my knees.
My green heels lock on a crossbar.
Blue mirrors seduce the words I am about
to model with blue lips
to rough companionable men whose dirty hands
talk loud around the bar.

"Here's from Harry." The barkeep slides me
a beer.
I raise the glass to Harry, and I say, thanks, Harry.

But I cannot say a name that's not my own.
I am not Pat or Doris
daytimes
and I am not a waitress with time off
a secretary, typist, or hairdresser,
and I don't sell.
I give my own number.

Beer comes around again. I raise
the glass to Sam, and I say, thanks, Sam.

"I'll take the Mack." "Hell, I'll take the Jimmy
anyday. Talk about trucks."
"Talk about engines."
"What's the life of a U-drive?"

41

When beer comes around again I raise the glass
to Bob, who drives a 33 Rolls Royce.

"Fuck the Chevrolet," Jack says,
and I smile, I smile
making my eyes dimple at that word.
Bob and Harry eye me past their beer.
But that word.
The mirror rocks.
"O, excuse me," says Jack, and

I have elbows. My body is bony.
My hair strings on my ears.
My dress is too big. I have small eyes.
My stomach bulges. My breath is yellow.
My box is made of tin.
My breasts are a pair of sneakers.

"Excuse me," says Jack.
And it's no good, it's no good ever.
I don't fuck.
I'm a different kind of whore.

Brackets

me wincing from a spine of light
splitting my braced blades

scrambling up highland pumice flats
from the pebbled racket of the sun

and from the outreach of his longfingered hands
he pacing me, lank and steady

his legs were a diagram of strings
I never fronted

        cleft I fell

pitched into a bracketed cell
which exhaled heavily mortal air

limp and agile as an ape I climbed ladders
listening to dark breath pulse under the rungs hanging

and swung onto the black catwalk
railing before huge doors with bony locks

beneath me I saw him drag and wind cord
about a boy's light body

and caught up an iron candelabrum
to hurl down to murder and save

but I could not let go armed
armed with candles without light

arms moving like weeds in the sea
dragged forward in a tidal pull and swimming

I could not drop the brachiate iron on the rankle
the coiler of cord who was hurting the boy

therefore I faced the great gates
stood the unlit candles aside

cast the laborious bolt
and heaved the panels outward

wailing to the apricot brilliance
from the darkness I shut behind me

my cowardice my failing my loss

Paper Boy

for Mead

He wakes up when the papers come, at four,
and rolls out of his hammock into the black air
that, having folded around him all night, now falls away
as he fumbles with the binding wire.
By remotely shining streetlights
he piles the papers, snaps on the rubber bands,
and packs his canvas bag.
The scooped moon is his fellow.
He turns to her with a strange sensation of trust.
She streams upon his unexpressive eyes.
As he swings the bag to his shoulders
they set off together carrying news up the mountain.

Morning begins to color the eastern reaches.
The moon pales. He yawns. The slack bag slips to the ground.
He lays himself flat on the grass
propping his head on the bag.
Light widens under his gaze.
Light, more light at the edges of heaven!
The streetlight fixes his eyes.
Inside the glassy chamber glows the point.
Staring, he dreams his passing into the glass.
Beyond the glass! He is free inside the chamber!
He is the filament. He is the light burning,
and brightness is loosed
that spreads out and moves, comprehensive,
over the whole world, about to be undone,
shining, shining.

Catching Sight of Wall Street in a Peculiar Light, I Am Flooded with Images out of the Past

The sunlight sifts in cinders over Wall Street,
And sudden images out of the old war
Streak into mind: The late Atlantic Fleet
Out on the Hudson, flat as paper, more
Idea than steel, even then; the oracular beat
Of armies crossing borders; the gun color,
The leaden fact, the vague figure of wind
That war assumes in a child's timeless mind.

A present sense of war is hard to keep:
I watch the immutable map of Europe shift;
When Paris falls, I falter, shocked, and weep;
I pray for the sturdy Dunkirk boats a swift
And lucky crossing; newsreel searchlights sweep
The staggered sky till there are no shadows left.
On American beaches only flecks of tar
From stricken subs and tankers tell of war.

But the air feels massive with hazard from the East,
The pioneer night, heroic with blackout. Day,
Severe in olive and navy, wears a cast
Of dream for all its drab.
                              If I found a way
When young to transform the murderous holocaust,
It was I knew Heaven would not allow the decay
Of Truth. Older than I, a generation died
For the victim Jews, for history, God on our side.

Truth triumphed. Out of the welter of bodies churned
In flaming oil off the coast of Iceland, out
Of the rubble of London, out of Hiroshima burned

Vermillion, the one thing left alive a spout
Of water from a broken iron pipe, I learned
That truth is mixed with falsehood, belief with doubt,
We are Jew and Nazi both. Guilty, forgiven,
We suffer, we live. Iron and broken, we live.

I live, dreaming my childhood, dreaming that war,
As I stand in Wall Street, where I first heard of the blast
That felled Hiroshima. Both seem less simple, far
More human than I knew, their heroes cast
To history with their knaves. They live, this hour
Ambiguous with their lives. We change the past
By understanding it. Memories of my youth,
Sunbeams in cinders, sift their way toward truth.

Gifts

I said silk. Years ago. I mean stone.
I said silk for shadows under it my body made—
Guessed rivulets, scoop of tipped lilies, green hollows.
I became, losing my soul in the fabric's fluid,
Undine. He kissed water. I inhabited the weedy shade
His hands wavered in for a while, till I deepened away.

I said language. I mean stone. I asked for words—
Distillations of lunacy the dry rage made
Flickering in his veins at night. Years ago.
I was the burned energy of his pages. I flamed
As radiant as he made me there, and as pure.
I rose in tongues. It was the words stayed.

I said jewels, treasure of earth. I mean stone. Quiet things
Recognized even in the ignorant hand, color
And weight and value of the light they cast,
Or more casually, not for themselves prized,
But for how they bind promises. Years ago, Yet I hardened
At last into indifferent elements, leaving jewels.

I said time. I mean stone. Loss of beauty, wealth and letters
Drew me to time, that matter of space and air
Which seems nothing and is all we have or change it to—
Measures of dark and bright, races, breath
And warm fragrances, cries of hurt or pleasure. Years ago.
Time became hope and then memory as it will forever.

He loves me still. I say stone. I mean stone.
Fire, fluid silk, earth's jewels, the breath of time it contains.
Years now. I say stone. I mean stone.

Losing

Love sifting out of mind
Eyes paling
Coils of the voice lost
The clear words turning less to less
All the hard bravery and risk wasting
The waited hands
The need gone that was
Pure signature of the rigged mood
The white and final weather
> *And I sang, Goodbye*
> *And I sang, midsummer come*
> *O salt in the wind*
> *O undiminishing danger.*

Naming Spring

one dream for Harry

I lay asleep in a lake of bright water
heavy slept an age
in the black silt
weighted as it shifted
and I did
wintering below cracked glass.

swelling the long outsurge of a
loosening reach beneath the limned leaves
letting go soft particle swirls that filmed
the dislodging lolling body rolling decomposed
to the broken surface.

and sheerly I am solved and saved in wet air
telling in hazardous clarity
at the steep waterbreak
shining things fractured at the open fall,
an illumination of unretractable words,
a spray of names.

The Divorce Poem

Say loss, trailing after a shade,
And you plunge into moonflakes
Blurring the high street of Madison,
And that's not what it was.

And it wasn't fucking in cornfields just,
In hot weather, or his big hand under your hair,
Or backyard kisses, the trillium sleeping near fences,
And late summer filling the kitchen.

It wasn't like that.

Say failure, the windows aggrieved,
The telephone costly with tears.
He was a man as moral as vegetables
And he made things work.

You didn't.
Say failure.
Say it.
Say the mark of ten years is a welt
You stagger feeling.

The Last Thing

What binds his raw wrists hard behind his back
is the last and hurtful thing he feels with his hands
in the chill air but the air itself,
as his fingers reach for his other hand.

He wants to hold at the last some familiar thing
like himself, but he can't lock his rigid fingers together.
His nakedness is his own pain,
white, and hard for him to carry.

The wind is like splinters in the gash on his shoulder,
bulging. Cracked blood stiffens the skin of his thigh
and the cold place he was mutilated—
Ache thickening in yellow bruises.

The grave at his feet is shallow. It is his own.
He dug it. Suddenly he will be clubbed into it.
Soon. And no friend will save him from it
at the very last. Nothing. No one.

He will die. The dying will not be long.
He can say, "Sara." He can say, "Lord Jesus."
"My country." "Good brothers, bless my death."
"Father." Whatever he chooses to say

is the last thing he will throw to the living air
from himself, and the enemy will hear but not understand.
Heavy to his neck the blow, back,
knees buckling, he falls, knocked

forward to the grave. "Sara!" He did not choose.
As he falls, he twists to break the fall with his shoulder.
Why break the fall? Had his head hit the stone
his shoulder struck, death would be easier.

Better this way, with the last and savage thoughts
as himself. Six minutes more. Earth. But harder.
The earth comes down on his back in lumps.
He closes his fingers around the earth

that he catches in his hands and holds. He is breathing.
The earth is falling. He can remember the earth—
the harrowed loam, ready for seed,
for the still seed. He has no seed.

Wheat. Hay. Barns. The brindled cow. Milk
pulled from her udder warm to the pail. Taste.
Earth in his mouth. His last breath,
and that full of flying dirt. Quick.

Sara. Elms. Apple blossoms. Rain. Wet hair.
The hunger for the apple on the bough
most out of reach. Earth. Earth.
The shape of him in earth unmoved.

It will not be hollow. Earth in the urgent jaw,
tongue, teeth, biting earth. Ladders. Apples.

Listening

The bridge glistens over the Bay
through a stammer of fog.
The hills are covered with wet light
dark and white buildings rise into.

Things you've said about loving me
collect and brim like still water
filling the brave declivities,
making them warm,
but your living voice in this city
would root up the cables, I think.
The stores and houses would get ripped apart if I saw,
somewhere in the slumbering corridors of these blue streets,
your back and arms,
your steady, familiar body.

Because I have not kept faith with you.

I never said anything about the rain of pure sound
dropping all around us,
spattering our shoulders and our grappling fingers
when we said goodbye,
and I did not speak of the sprung light in your face
which made what you meant distinct and particular
as our first harried kisses might be.

Evening in Bolinas

As the combers heave themselves this way
As the ocean exhales fog into these thickets
    I charge you with lost breath.

Fog hides the mild wane of color, itself gray.
Ochre on stalks of wild oat, flesh pink on amaryllis
Give themselves into half white.
I almost cannot see the cold waves of light
Approach and withdraw below along the cliff base,
Their huge sound reaching.
    I charge you with failure.

The road I came on has gone into the soft wall.
I know it leads back into other roads.
The ocean can hold whatever shifts of light or dark come in.
Beyond fog, beyond nightfall, beyond even air
The stars have come together for good
And do not turn from their ways.
    I charge you with a broken word.

Except for me, you have never been here.

three

In the speaking
                    leaves
Eve

Things You Will Never Have

Sweet pitch of white pine
sticks to my fingers from a cone
I picked up this morning. Rubbing
won't rid me of it. That's what I wanted.

I want that, and I want
this very romantic light falling on wings
of a blue jay in flight across a poplar,
sallow, trembling and fading.

I bless the leaves falling,
eddying, the red leaves, to earth,
to death and frosty grass.
I bless the lichen on oak bark. . . .

Listen: You can't have this.
Not this, or the dark stand of cedars,
or Norway maples, or white toadstools poking
out of moss under dead pine needles.

There are some things you cannot have—
not bayberry or deep sumac or birch,
none of these. Other things too—things
you want now, things you will never have.

Believe that. Walk into it as if it were lasting darkness.
There's no violation in such dark, and,
well, you can remember this vagrant and holy season
very clearly—there's that.

Midas

Six o'clock.
Between the police station and the children's hospital
A tree is fluttering.
The branches shake loose an eerie light
To sift upon the golden pharmacy
And the golden doctors' offices.
Birds with human tongues
Rake my hair, metallic wings swirling.
All my donkey secrets
Twist in their transparent feet.

This Night

This night
this of warm stars the koa widens into
was more than all others improbable five years ago.
I try to touch something for the sake of belief:
There's nothing between myself and the dark I reach
but need.
Answers I conjure
are as unlikely as these clamorous clouds
brightening without a moon
that raven on darkness.

Did I give myself ever?

And, if I did,
why do I not eat darkness now?

The aloe would prickle, not heal.
The barbed hala would scrape a throat
washed with the venomous milk of oleander.
Weakness could feed me on strange meals.
Therefore I will not eat.
What have I to do with hunger?

I will wear if I can the cool civility of the koa
whose leaves are like crescents of moon.
This tree of quiet
can still in its wide branches equally
distances of the wheeling constellations
or my own failed peace.

What are years, after all, when they are gone?
Time widens the dark tree.
I have reached this night.

Eve

the trees wrap their branches
and vines drop
unwinding out of
leaves, heavy, leaves thickening
to flutter in blood
the air is warm with serpents
muscles of slime
complex in innocent nerves they
braid their bright scales
by the fibres of my hair
my body
hangs in Eden
like a lily of milk
steaming with time
as I begin to fill
with the sick heat of memory
how shall I bless my Original?

Poetry

The quick breathing, the names in beaten air,
and, after that, the healing.
Then how can I live, and how long,
in a city filled over and over again with such words
and not tell you?

I went away
to draw those voices deeper in me.
I walked with my good friend
far into Iao Valley where mist slurs
the cold ridge of the pinnacle,
and gave him there
a white, erotic flower without a name, color
at the center of paling sun.
But this changed nothing.

He knew and left me
at the jagged edge of the stream
everlastingly dragged from the mountain down.
By a weathered flat rock in the stream bed,
I stripped and got into the water.
Rippling all around me on the sleeping stones,
it broke the other sky,
the sunny images of green leaves,
and fell away, light beading all over my arms
and around my body, hanging dream-cold, stone-held,
slapped over the loosening gravel,
until the names vanished in the sound.

And maybe everything we said
slid away in the heavy water.

I climbed to a rock
and watched the sunflecked skin become dry.
Late afternoon's diffuse light brought us back to the city.

In the air, a noise like breath rouses,
Word-shaped, like a speaking wind.
The images begin.
How long can I live and not tell you?

The Deep, the Quiet

You never say anything.

I reach into new places
Where water hurts,
And the still clarity of wristbones,
Their slender arcing,
Aches like spring snow, but softer.
Dark leaf shapes do not disintegrate
In the stirred silt,
But how far down things decay!
How the place brightens with cold!

I have said wrong things.
Deep in my breath they wait for me.
Shall I call them back?
They will come of themselves.

For love is a brightening
That stirs outward in rings
To the rims of the places it was laid in.
It is not wasted,
But in light ripples returns again.
My words may therefore diminish
But not fail.
They close to the center.

I keep you in a place so deep and lucid
You cannot be guessed.
From that quiet,
Inward as far as truth can be sounded,
Wells what I am, what you and the water are.
I do not live without you.

Like a Stone That Has Waited

Deeper now, my stillness must reach from
a space mined out in the last blight.
It lies densely collected inside
like a stone that has waited a long time to harden
annealed in the middle of gnarled fire
and shot with light.

Yet in that sealed silence
I feel the seried rings of your listening
stream around and around me
serenely exhaling
and it is you I safely wait for.

If a restless accidental sigh
should come from what more I need
do not veer to compassion: I will keep my stillness
longer than before.
But in things all time is equal.
I will perhaps therefore give you a stone

out of whose concentric purity
will shine luster of old suns
warmly disturbing the wideness between your breath
and my pulse.

The Doors and Windows

His words are
the familiar
                things
held safe
as lines
I hang on silent
all the while
                I think
                        strings
I think, sinews of his arms
tendons
strung over obsessive limbs
fibres of soft hair on his arms catching
shine of yellow light
in his attending eyes
                        joints hinging
and the long windows giving
upon brilliance of shaped clouds
upon the aqua windowed at his back
what color are his eyes?
and all the doors on their hinges wailing
semicircular wide
wailing on their hinges
The locks are sprung.
Swung wide on their hinges all the doors stand open.
I cannot tell the color of his eyes.

Rifts

Divisions: phrases of songs.
The periodic blue sweep of streetlights
Across windshield and steering wheel.

A wilderness of doors in the suburbs
Open on frank ambiguous voices
Dissolving to a stripped hosannah or lament.

This: the wet print of a leaf
Blown in upon the floor as I came in to see him,
His fingers on white keys.

Afterwards, if there was night,
There was rain also to darken the city
And make the highway shine obscurely.

Phrases of songs, the cloudy pulling on
Of white cars. And away.

Love without a Talisman

Times your big fingers smear the tears you've brought me to—
not you, really, the loss of you,
not that even—it's remembering I loved you
and that I don't
makes me waver,
a shade in water stirred—
I need something to touch.

You'd think my hands might remember
ridges of ear—
yet they don't—
warm turns of the shoulder
hipline
arc of the fluid groin.
Abstract.
They softly dissolve.
I can touch nothing.
What did I love?

Hater of gifts, you offered me out of this wreck
nothing to save, so there's no way back
in a copper stone
to the sun abandoned on pebbles
of a red Lake Michigan harbor,
in the pocked hollow bone of a bird
to the whistle of love,
in a ring to a promise of snow.
Cold.
All you ever gave me was your body.
There's nothing to hold.

I Have No Eyes

for Mead, William and John

In the bare silence of the main,
Can starlight, laddering salt water,
Shudder deep into what sightless creature
Hangs there? To matter, I mean,
To make a difference to those locked eyes?

If we, weighted by the sea,
Tonight tried finding under ocean
Roads by the moon—
Though the moon blazon snowy light in heaven
Or turn blood mad, eclipsed,
We might, feeling on our muscles the swell of tides,
Sense the sound of a passage
But not see a way:
Feeling is what we know.

I know my life hurts you.
Though I love you, loved you first,
Bore you inward, my sons,
Held in my black sockets your images, upside down,
I would have done the same, anyway, that I have done—
Sounded out, as truly as I could, fair passage,
Discovering false by false feeling, changed.

Vibrations of light, even sunlight,
Make no sound in water.
They come from so far.
And O, listen, I have no eyes.

Banyan Roots

for Frank and Susan

In this dark
        the nervous roots are awake
tangling in blown air.
                    They distend, aching
toward sweet dirt,
            sparely—
banyan fibres, hair
            loosening
twisting again, fingers
roping around the trunk,
yearning out of the wrung sockets
where the bark
            wrinkles a little.
In this dark
the tree's breath warms a wilderness beneath
spreads open, entirely tender,
and will find for the groping radicals
                    not yet
soft places in earth.

More than Light

i.

What more than light sleeping
in the runnels of these woods
troubles the deep shade?
This world seems other.

The ground sleeps
that holds the sleeping, sodden.
The leaves rouse. Even this air
is of the past.

Lives of small animals are scattering
in front of something. Their breaths
hurt them. They are afraid of seeds.
I fear the fall of leaves, not less.

O dark and water, keep me. But not here.
To love nothing is safe.
What's possible is released in cries
to the assaulting air. Who's near?

ii.

What shade of light
wakening in mere water rises easily
and, from the strict arcs of his wrists
shakes off in wet rings manacles of sleep?

Water-weeds shimmer in this merciless changing.
Listening things abandon themselves to stillness.
What more than light and how he carries it
spills from the torn water toward the stones?

Danger begins in reflections where branches
lean through the planes. He slips his snares!
Arrested—all leaves, seeds, breath yielded—
all taken! And he at ease.

Risen, he harries his catch
translating what he touches with desire.
Though I come less to love
than he comes to life from slumber, I come.

Listening in these woods that want
my own sound, I hear water, hear
dull pebbles, hear crying
with nothing to hold.

Yet I am held, warm to his
fingers, hands, arms, shoulders, eyes.
Though I faltered, here is light, only light,
bursting, fragmented light, light

hurled everywhere, light burning on everything,
blessing and ruining what it illumines.
Someone has risen here into more than light
who will never sleep again in the world I come to.

Waiting for Snow

White of ash is the light bark of the trees that are waiting
For snow
(Ash color on the charred sky of winter)
With a stillness so absolute
That they, who are strong, seem frail.
They do not shiver.
They are attentive and mild, even,
Not listening, waiting only,
Ready and bare.
The snow when it falls will not be harsh with them I know
Who have driven this way every day slowly
Because of them, because I thought
That if by looking at them from afar I could understand
How they carry their heavy branches,
I could temper my hope,
If the hard weather lasts.

I think it was not the cruelty of the season
Made them stand like this without stirring.
For they answered with anger the ruinous wind
That fell on them early this month under the humped moon
Stripping their leaves.
They are not now submissive.
It's open they are, and passive.
The way they wait is like the way they wore their green
In the sweet, warm air of summer,
All that abundance not alien to them.
They did not swagger then for their riches,
And in winter they are not ashamed of being naked.

I don't think their simpleness comes from battling hail.
Anyone can rage splendidly on a bitten field.

It's carrying leaves or standing stripped of them,
Knowing the fibre inside and always the cellular streaming of water
And being sure of hardness in the heartwood—these matter.
These keep them from being derelict or weather-broken as they wait
For snow
That spreads their branches wider
And, masking them,
Makes them witnesses who gravely acknowledge
What they already unresistingly are.

My Name Sleeps at the River's Edge

Even these walls are not indifferent
When I come in.
You are not here yet.
The hasps of the sliding windows
Need to be lifted
So I can admit the bright midday,
The smell of brine.

How many hours!
How many hours since, was it,
I waited for you to speak my name?

> My name is a leaf
> That sleeps with yours between stones
> I placed at the river's edge last spring
> Believing gods of that valley
> Could bring me to your arms' circle
> Your warm breath to my hair
> Telling me and untelling
> Me who I am.

Sea light drifts to this
Room full of rugs, tables, blank photographs
And air conditioning, and the whole apartment
Begins to drown in the astounding colors of salt water.
You come in, a drowning man.
Your hands reach from the flood.
Your breath struggles in my hair to save us.

Save us! Call me by name!
And more. Take me to the river's edge
And waken me there.

You can't save us here. These deeps
Are only the sea light I let in from outside.
Nothing matters here.
Name things as you will,
This room is imaginary.
You risk nothing. Even if you drown
It will be as if it had never happened.

Yet at the river's edge
My name sleeps, a leaf under altar stones.
Oh, in that valley, tell me who I am!
I crave the taste of my name there
Warm in your mouth,
Your breath moist at my ear.

Driving to the Cold Hollow Mountains

for Geoff Hewitt

Strayed on the wide roads that drive north into Canada,
I've been drummed all day into the pitched colors
of the leaves dying. Times over, many times,
I found my hand a hard fist on the steering wheel
and my throat harsh with swallowing salt
in my laughter, love scraping the soaked air
for the trees
that declare their own bright translation
to the white houses and the weathered barns
they've lived next to all year.

For God's seal is on the trees:
They're going crazy in crowds by immovable boulders
and huge wet outcrops of granite.
They're going crazy with others in meadows stiff with gold weeds
or going crazy alone in certain patches of land
stretched fallow beside the black highways.
They go staggering, headlong exaltations of light,
as if God were asking in the red leaves
that shatter with visible rage the flared blue sky:
Where wast thou when I laid the foundations of the earth?

I grant I was not here,
that I have no understanding of these changes.
Things happen.
I don't ask for answers any more,
but I have not learned how to suffer without noise
anything
even illuminations of dead leaves.

Nevertheless, if this is how things fall apart,
then let the Last Day come
beating on the ruddy hillsides,
bearing God's seal to hurt not the trees,
His last seal
which is silence.

Muir Woods

Afternoon: we lie here on our backs
in sunlight heavy enough to break
through dense wheels of upper branches
and fall down the moody redwood trunks.
(When will we kiss? Will we?) Dark
needles
under our bodies;
ferns, as soft as they, green
as sun
upon the burned out black
charcoal caves in the trees.
(Our arms lie close, but our hands do not touch—
each
a separate body.)
The massive, ravaged bodies of the trees
make a circle.
Is this a temple?
(Is this
why we do not kiss?)
God-rooted in love
limned in this evergreen grove,
I stare upward, where sunlight is spitted
gold on charred sticks.
I raise both arms
together, straight along the steep lines
of the trees'
tough muscles, feeling my self into them.
And those dread, immense lives

                                       seize

mine
into their double selves.

I harden tall. I have risen
a shaft of amber
in a red forest circle
where the brilliant spill of sunlight is allayed
as my boughs turn gently and spread
to bear new seed cones
in shaded places.
We will not kiss.
The redwoods circle us.
We have grown roots and branches of their peace.

Daphne

Winter: hoarse, oracular.
The rain stings, suicidally bitter, like desire.
Why must my legs be bare
All the way up my thighs, cold,
And my soles wet?

Stench of soft bark.
On my fiingers the scent of laurel crushed
Freshens, but it does not heal
The darkness in the mind's
Pith.

How did the summer fail?
He placed mouth
Upon my ear.
His warm breath
Moistened my hair.
I heard a god exhale.

But now the haggard wind circling my head
Rasps in burned redwood.
Plagues spring in his stride.
Am I raving? I felt healed.
The heavy wind that breathes in these soaked trees
Rattles through me. I'm cold.
I think I have eaten with the dead.
I'm cold.
Wrenched against his intelligent body
I have seen bay branches with his eyes.

They are stripped. They are wet.
They shiver a little, stiffly.
They do not grow very high.

They are darker than all the green around them.
The leaves have tiny waves on the edges like
A smile of wind.
A god might mark them, quiet them,
Move in what is open
Of these laurel leaves
Most tenderly.